Build a
Compost Tumbler

BY TRACY ABELL · ILLUSTRATED BY ROGER STEWART

The Child's World®
childsworld.com

Published by The Child's World®
1980 Lookout Drive · Mankato, MN 56003-1705
800-599-READ · www.childsworld.com

Acknowledgments
The Child's World®: Mary Swensen, Publishing Director
Red Line Editorial: Editorial direction and production
The Design Lab: Design

Photographs ©: iStockphoto, 4; Sergey Zavalnyuk/iStockphoto, 5;
Stephan Zabel/iStockphoto, 6; Shutterstock Images, 7, 8, 9

Design Elements: JosephTodaro/Texturevault; Shutterstock Images

ISBN 9781503807853

LCCN 2015958129

Printed in the United States of America
Mankato, MN
June, 2016
PA02301

ABOUT THE AUTHOR

Tracy Abell lives in the foothills of the Rocky Mountains, where she composts in her backyard. So far, she has one compost box and one tumbler, and she is thinking about having a worm bin inside her home.

ABOUT THE ILLUSTRATOR

Roger Stewart has been an artist and illustrator for more than 30 years. His first job involved drawing aircraft parts. Since then, he has worked in advertising, design, film, and publishing. Roger has lived in London, England, and Sydney, Australia, but he now lives on the southern coast of England.

Contents

CHAPTER ONE
NATURE'S RECYCLING PROGRAM, 4

CHAPTER TWO
GOOD FOR NATURE AND PEOPLE, 6

CHAPTER THREE
COMPOST TUMBLERS, 8

CHAPTER FOUR
BUILDING A COMPOST TUMBLER, 10

Glossary, 22

To Learn More, 23

Index, 24

Nature's Recycling Program

Composting is nature's **recycling** program. Think about a leafy forest. The leaves drop to the ground in fall. They pile up. They mix with dead plants and animal waste. These things slowly break down. Small **organisms** help. Some of the material gets turned into gas. **Minerals** from the dead material go into the soil. The dead material is gone by spring. The soil is rich. The minerals help new plants grow. Everything gets reused. People can compost, too. We can reuse things we would

In nature, mushrooms help break down dead material.

normally throw away. About 25 percent of waste in the United States can be composted. This includes things such as yard waste and food scraps. Things people throw away go to **landfills**. It can take a long time for waste to break down in these places. When we compost, waste does not go to the landfill. We keep it in one spot. We do things to help organisms break it down. It becomes dark and crumbly. This substance is called compost. It is full of minerals. We can add it to a garden to help plants grow.

Waste in landfills breaks down very slowly.

CHAPTER TWO

Good for Nature and People

Plants need good soil to grow. Sometimes soil is too loose and sandy. Water washes it away. Adding compost helps loose soil stick together and stay in place. Other times, soil is packed too thick. Compost loosens up thick soil. It allows more water and air to enter. This means the soil does not need to be watered as much.

Soil with compost also stores more minerals. Minerals help plants stay healthy. But they also benefit people. When we eat plants, we take in their minerals. Some people use

Dry soil can wash away. It does not give plants what they need to grow strong and healthy.

Compost helps soil become dark and rich.

fertilizer to help make soil richer. But these chemicals can run into water supplies. They can make animals sick. Compost is a natural fertilizer. It slowly puts minerals into the soil. It also contains organisms that are good for soil. These organisms also help keep pests away from plants. Composting can save people money on chemicals for their plants.

Composting also keeps waste from going to landfills. In landfills, the materials get broken down in a different way. The process makes a gas called methane. This gas is bad for our environment. It traps heat. This adds to **climate change**. Composting does not release this gas.

CHAPTER THREE

Compost Tumblers

Compost tumblers come in many shapes and sizes.

Using a tumbler is a great way to compost. Tumblers are barrels people put their waste in. Organisms live in the tumbler. They break down the materials. But as they do, they need oxygen. This is where the tumbler comes in. Spinning the barrel moves everything inside. It gives the organisms more oxygen. They keep working. The process gives off heat. You can tell a tumbler is working when it warms up.

People like composting with tumblers for many reasons. Tumblers are easy to turn. They hide the messy pile of waste. They keep mice and pests out. And bad smells stay inside the barrel.

Some people compost with bins. Bins make it more difficult to move the material inside.

WHEN IS IT READY?

There are a few signs your compost is close to being ready. It will not heat up as much when you turn the barrel. It will not look like the things you put in. It will be dark and crumbly. Good compost also has an earthy smell. You can test the smell. Put some material in a sealed bag. Let it sit for a few days. If it has the same earthy smell after a few days, it is ready. It is not ready if it smells rotten.

Using a tumbler can speed up composting. But it is still a slow process. People collect waste over weeks to add to their tumblers. Most people spin their tumblers every two or three days. They stop adding material when their tumblers are mostly full. After this, it can take months for the material to be ready. The big benefits to the garden and nature are worth the wait!

CHAPTER FOUR

Building a Compost Tumbler

Making compost is easy. First, you need to gather materials to build your tumbler. You can reuse materials to make it. For example, you might use scrap wood instead of two-by-fours. Or you could use old skateboard wheels for the rollers on your tumbler. You might even be able to reuse a barrel. You can ask food or beverage distributors whether they have any extra barrels.

Next, start gathering materials to put into your tumbler. You will need two kinds: greens and browns. Greens are things such as fruits, vegetables, eggshells, tea bags, bread, and coffee grounds and filters. Grass clippings, young weeds, and pet fur are also greens. Browns include dead leaves, straw, sticks and twigs, newspaper, cereal boxes, paper plates, and cardboard. Keep your greens and browns separate until they go in the tumbler.

MATERIALS

- ☐ 2 two-by-fours cut to the length of the barrel
- ☐ Measuring tape
- ☐ Pencil
- ☐ 2 two-by-fours cut to the width of the barrel
- ☐ 16 2.5-inch (6.4 cm) wood screws
- ☐ Handheld cordless drill
- ☐ 55-gallon (210 L) plastic barrel with removable lid

- ☐ 4 3-inch (8 cm) fixed casters
- ☐ 16 1.5-inch (3.8 cm) wood screws
- ☐ Green material
- ☐ Brown material
- ☐ Soil
- ☐ Shovel
- ☐ Garden hose or watering can

DEAD LEAVES

You can compost dead leaves by themselves. Have an adult help make a small fenced-in area to hold the leaves. Dump leaves into the holder. Pack them down. Add water to the pile each time you add leaves. Let the pile sit. After a year or two, you will have leaf compost.

INSTRUCTIONS

STEP 1: Lay the two longer boards face down next to each other. Space them out.

STEP 2: Measure 6 inches (15 cm) from each end of both boards. Mark the measurements.

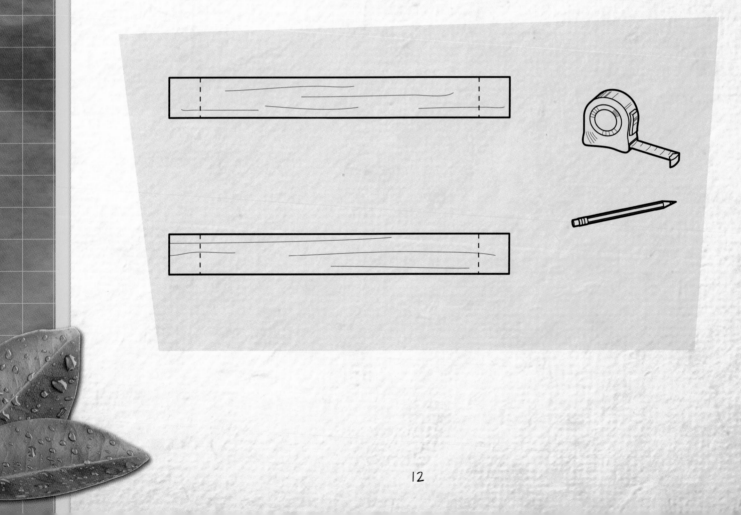

STEP 3: Place the outside edges of the shorter boards where you made the marks. The shorter boards should span between the longer ones. This will make a rectangle.

STEP 4: Use the drill to connect the boards with 2.5-inch (6.4 cm) screws. Use four screws at each place the boards meet. This is your platform.

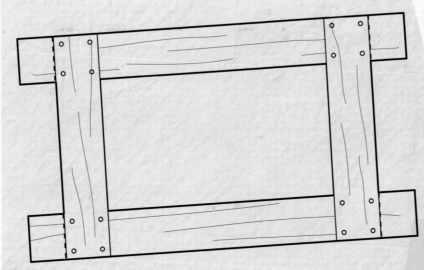

STEP 5: Have one or two people hold the barrel over the platform. It should be about 2 inches (5 cm) above the boards. One at a time, move each caster into place. Slide each one along the center of the shorter boards. Stop when the wheel touches the barrel. Mark the position. Draw a circle in each screw hole. The wheels should form a rectangle.

ROLL TEST

At first, put only two screws in each caster. Test the wheel location. Place the barrel on the wheels and roll it. The wheels might be not quite in the right place. The barrel might not roll smoothly. Or it might drift to one side. You may need to move the wheels. Drilling only two screws at a time means there will not be as many screws to take out.

STEP 6: Set the barrel aside. Use the marks you made on the platform as guides. Take the 1.5-inch (3.8 cm) wood screws. Use the drill to screw the wheels to the boards.

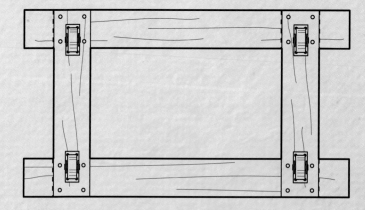

STEP 7: Have an adult drill 20 to 30 holes into the sides and bottom of the barrel. Use a .5-inch (1.3 cm) drill bit.

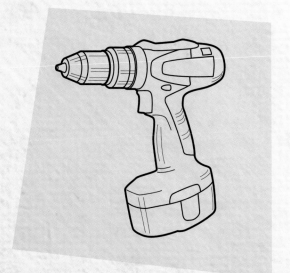

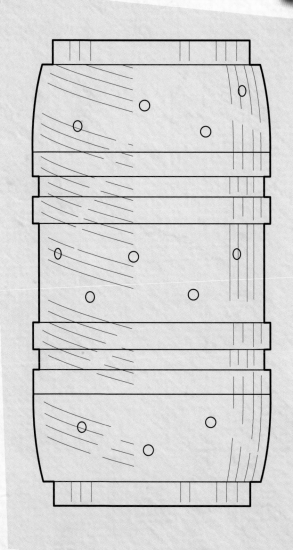

STEP 8: Place your collected greens and browns in piles. Make a third pile of soil.

STEP 9: Place the barrel on the wheels. Open the lid. Add materials in layers. Begin with a layer of soil to get started. Add a layer of browns. Add a layer of greens. Make the brown layer twice as thick as the green layer. Take the garden hose or watering can. Wet each layer before adding another.

STEP 10: Put the lid on. Turn the tumbler.

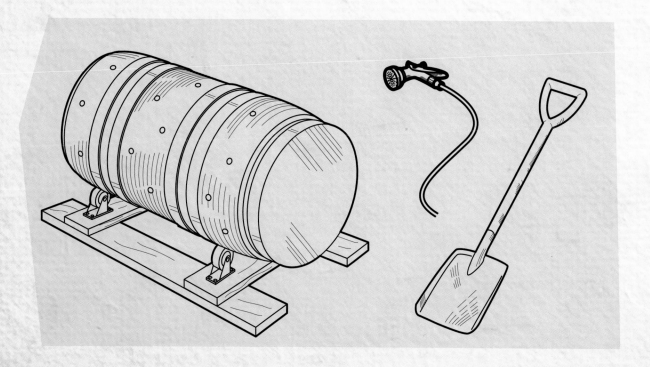

STEP 11: Continue to add material to the tumbler until it is at least half full. Then, stop adding new material. Wait for your waste to turn into compost. Check on and spin your tumbler at least a couple times per week.

STEP 12: Once the material has turned to compost, take it out of the tumbler. Use it in a home or community garden. Spread at least 1 inch (2.5 cm) of compost on top of the soil.

POSSIBLE PROBLEMS

Your tumbler might start to smell bad. This may mean it is too wet. Try adding browns to the top. Turn the tumbler. The material inside should feel like a squeezed out sponge. Your tumbler might also attract a lot of flies. This may be because food scraps are not mixed in well enough. Try mixing them in more and turning your tumbler.

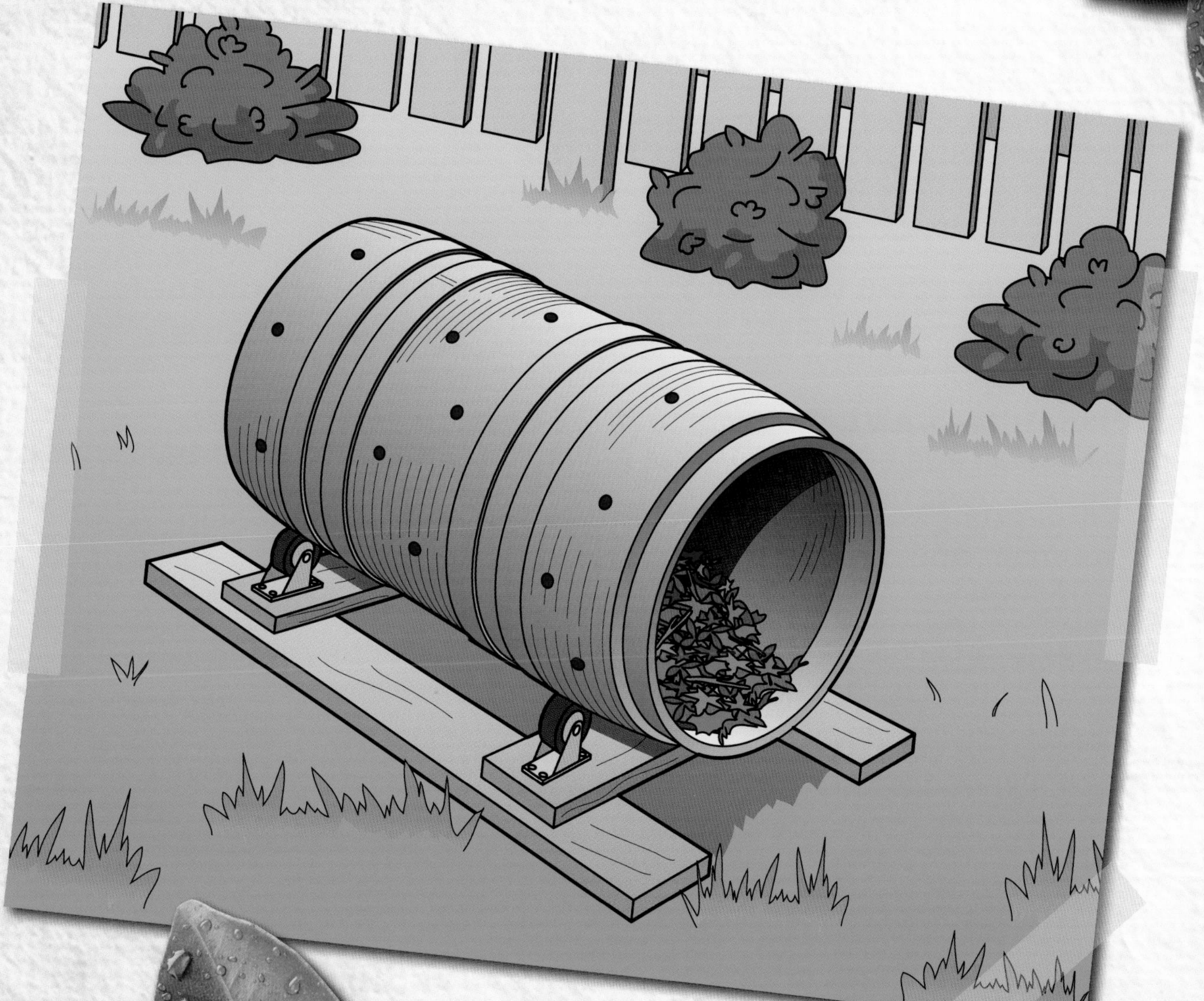

GLOSSARY

climate change (KLYE-mit CHAYNJ) Climate change is when there is a big change in the weather over a long period of time. Pollution in the air helps cause climate change.

fertilizer (FUR-tu-lize-ur) Fertilizer is a natural or human-made substance used to make soil richer. Fertilizer helps plants grow strong and healthy.

landfills (LAND-fils) Landfills are places where garbage is collected and buried. Material in landfills breaks down slowly.

minerals (MIN-ur-uls) Minerals are compounds that help plants, animals, and humans be healthy. Plants use their roots to take up minerals.

organisms (OR-gu-niz-ums) Organisms are living things. Bacteria are organisms that help the composting process.

recycling (ree-SY-kul-ing) Recycling is changing waste so it can be used again. Most major cities have curbside recycling programs.

TO LEARN MORE

In the Library

Aloian, Molly. *Green Gardening and Composting*.
New York: Crabtree, 2014.

Barker, David. *Compost It*. Ann Arbor, MI: Cherry Lake, 2010.

Martin, Jacqueline Briggs. *Farmer Will Allen and the Growing
Table*. Pine Plains, NY: Live Oak, 2014.

On the Web

Visit our Web site for links about
compost tumblers:
childsworld.com/links

*Note to Parents, Teachers, and Librarians:
We routinely verify our Web links to make sure
they are safe and active sites. So encourage
your readers to check them out!*

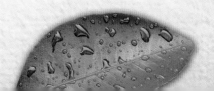

INDEX

barrel, 8-9, 10-11, 15, 16-17, 19
browns, 10-11, 18-19, 20

caster, 11, 15, 16
chemicals, 7
climate change, 7
compost (material), 5, 6-7, 9, 10, 20

fertilizer, 7
food scraps, 5, 20

greens, 10-11, 18-19

landfills, 5, 7
leaves, 4, 10-11

methane, 7
minerals, 4-5, 6-7

organisms, 4-5, 7, 8
oxygen, 8

pests, 7, 8,
plants, 4-5, 6-7

recycling, 4
reuse, 4, 10

soil, 4, 6-7, 11, 18-19, 20

tumbler, 8-9, 10, 19, 20
two-by-four, 10-11

waste, 4-5, 7, 8-9

yard waste, 5